GREATNESS RISES IN EACH NEW DAY

KATIE FALKOWSKI

Copyright © 2016 Katie Falkowski.

All Rights Reserved. No part(s) of this book may be reproduced, distributed or transmitted in any form, or by any means, or stored in a database or retrieval systems without prior expressed written permission of the author of this book.

ISBN: 978-1-62217-836-0

Acknowledgments

"Profound responsibilities come with teaching and coaching. You can do so much good- or harm. It's why I believe that next to parenting, teaching and coaching are the two most important professions in the world."
-Coach John Wooden

I have been blessed beyond measure with amazing parents, teachers, and coaches throughout my life. I am immensely grateful to them for guiding me in the right direction and helping me become the woman that I am today.

To my parents who have always given me their unwavering support and belief, thank you for your selfless example and endless love.

To my grade school and high school teachers, thank you for giving me a solid foundation upon which to build my future.

To my professors and mentors during my years spent at Holy Cross and Creighton, thank you for allowing me to explore my interests and follow my heart.

To my students who experienced first hand my trial by fire, thank you for your patience, your humor, and for teaching me more than I ever taught you.

To my coaches from preschool t-ball to college hockey, especially Jeffrey Oliver, thank you for teaching me the value of being scrappy, embracing challenges, and understanding the value of teamwork.

"Keep away from those who try to belittle your ambitions. Small people always do that, but the really great make you believe that you too can become great."
– Mark Twain

My life has been full of great friends and communities who have shared in my struggles and my victories, have made me laugh, and perhaps most importantly believed that I could become great.

To my mentors, particularly during my time in Rapid City, South Dakota, thank you for taking me under your wings, teaching me the true meaning of hospitality, and for creating a new home for me when I was half a country away.

To my friends throughout the years, thank you for the endless laughter, amazing memories, and for journeying with me as I wandered in the direction of my calling.

To Erik, thank you for reminding me every day that I am strong and beautiful, for supporting me in everything that I do, and for putting up with my craziness and hanger.

To the CrossFit Hyannis community, thank you for believing in me and letting me be part of your journey- you inspire and motivate me every day.

And to all those who have influenced and believed in me over the years, thank you for pointing me in the right direction, supporting my endeavors, and being part of my journey.

To all those who aren't afraid to pursue their goals with grit, determination, and an indomitable spirit.
Keep grinding.

"Because when we sit down day after day and keep grinding, something mysterious starts to happen. A process is set into motion by which, inevitably and infallibly, heaven comes to our aid. Unseen forces enlist in our cause; serendipity reinforces our purpose."

-Steven Pressfield, "The War of Art"

"Until one is committed, there is hesitancy, the chance to draw back. Concerning all acts of initiative (and creation), there is one elementary truth, the ignorance of which kills countless ideas and splendid plans: that the moment one definitely commits oneself, then Providence moves too. All sorts of things occur to help one that would never otherwise have occurred. A whole stream of events issues from the decision, raising in one's favor all manner of unforeseen incidents and meetings and material assistance, which no man could have dreamed would have come his way.

Whatever you can do, or dream you can do, begin it. Boldness has genius, power, and magic in it. Begin it now."

-W.H. Murray

Contents

Acknowledgments iii
Introduction. 1
Live Your Dream 7
Virtuosity in Everyday Life. 14
You Are Who You Want to Become 19
Get Your Shit Together 23
Make Today the Best Day Ever. 27
Everything Happens for a Reason. 31
Embrace Being Scrappy 35
A Universal Resolution. 40
I Just Got Better. 44
Sisu—Strength in Adversity 49
Make Tomorrow Your Lucky Day 53
Don't Wish It Away 57
Transformative Love. 61
Passionately Pursue Your Goals 65
Big Commit. 69
Just Keep Moving. 73
Fear Not. 77
Haters Gonna Hate 81
Come Back. 86
Choose To Be Happy, Choose To Be You .. 91
Hunt Down Opportunity - Say Yes 96
Fake It 'Til You Make It 101
The Golden Rule 105
Just a Scrapper Livin' the Dream 109
About the Author. 125

Introduction

YES, GREATNESS IS AVAILABLE FOR the taking. You and your life can be, and should be, truly great.

But here's the thing—you have to show up. You have to get out of bed, get away from the doubts in your head, and you have to show up. Show up, listen and learn, and be willing to work hard. Do these things and greatness is within your reach, likely closer than you thought possible. Does this seem too easy; is it a trick? No. Get up, show up, and grind—greatness will be on the other end of your efforts.

Over the last several years in teaching, coaching, and observing people's varying levels of success in different endeavors, I've noticed that this premise of showing up and putting in work has proven to be the difference between those who attain success and those who fall short. I truly believe that we are capable of achieving greatness in our personal, professional, and social lives—but it doesn't necessarily come easily. That being said, however, the first step toward greatness seemingly isn't that hard either—JUST SHOW UP. And yet time after time, I see people who refuse to take the first step. Perhaps they are afraid of a possible negative outcome, embarrassing themselves, or never reaching the goal that they set out for. Maybe they fear what others will think of them if they go after what they want and don't succeed (or do). Whatever the reason, many people quit before they even start. News flash—you're not going anywhere if you don't ever start. Obvious, right?

Over the last four plus years as a gym owner, I can't tell you how many times I have uttered the words "just show up." I know that when people set foot into my gym for a workout and do what I ask of them, they will leave better than when they walked in, and one step closer to their fitness goals. In many regards, I take the thinking out of it for them. Show up and do what I say with your full effort and you'll see results. And yet even after assuring people that they can reach their goals if they simply walk through the doors and work to the best of their abilities, still people choose not to take the first step (or perhaps take that first step but stop once it becomes too hard). We can't shy away from our fear. Acknowledge it, sure. But don't let it stop you from beginning the work that you set out to do. And never let it stop you once you get rolling. There will be doubts along the way, no matter what journey it is you are embarking on, but you just have to keep showing up and putting in smart, hard work.

I see this daily in the fitness world, but this concept holds true in most of life's endeavors. A friend of mine is a carpenter by trade and recently started his own construction company. Within the first year, his business went from one employee to nearly twenty, and grossed over one million dollars. He has work coming to him in every direction, and his business is showing extraordinary growth each day. How did he do it? He wakes up at 5:00am nearly everyday (including weekends) and starts the GRIND. He makes phone calls, checks on his jobs, manages his employees, gets new customers, and regularly works on the growth of his business. In short, he does not shy away from hard work. The most challenging thing for him? Finding employees who are willing to show up on time and do what they are hired, and paid well, to do. In a time where many complain that they can't find jobs, his criteria for hire is that you show up on time and you do the work you are told to do. There is no need to be a master carpenter. He will teach you the skills you need to do to get the job done. Sometimes it is as simple as taking trash to the dumpster and helping organize job sites, and yet finding people who are willing to show up and work is incredibly challenging.

The premise remains the same no matter the level, from high school students in their first job to CEOs of major companies—in order to find success, you have to be willing to put in work. My first job when I was in high school was working at a local sporting goods store. I was the only female employee amidst a brood of high school boys, and I was constantly praised by the managers for what a great job I was doing. This baffled me, as I didn't consider what I was doing to be anything special. I showed up on time, helped customers, tidied up, put out inventory, sharpened skates, and did whatever other small tasks I was asked to do. What was the difference between me and the other employees? I showed up and worked. It was that simple. None of the jobs were particularly challenging, but I understood that it was my responsibility to do them even if my boss wasn't looming over my shoulder. That job set me up for all the jobs I had moving forward and gave me an early understanding of the importance of showing up and working hard, even if the job seems menial.

Get up, show up, and GRIND. Greatness awaits you. When you live the GRIND it means you are never afraid to work for what you want, refuse to settle for the status quo, and constantly pursue excellence and greatness. The GRIND is a lifestyle, and it's one to be embraced.

But what is greatness? Greatness looks different for different people, but ultimately greatness means becoming the best version of yourself in all that you do. It's a commitment to bettering yourself each day and living a life of satisfaction and joy.

Many people fear that they can never be great or live the lives they desire, so they don't ever start working toward it. They find excuses for why things are too hard, or why they could never attain what they truly want. Know that you are capable of greatness and will achieve it, but only if you put your best foot forward. The best version of yourself is capable of greatness, and that's what you (and the world) deserve. But if you never show up or commit, chances are you'll never reach your full potential.

I realize that many people shy away from or poke fun at "self help" books, thinking that they already have all the answers and don't need someone else to motivate them or tell them what to do to be successful. And although I suppose you could call this a "self help" book, the reality is that most of the lessons within it are things you already inherently know but may have forgotten along the way. It's inevitable that at different times in our lives we're all going to need a little help getting on the right track and working toward being our best selves. This book is simply meant to help and inspire you to do that, and to realize your full potential.

"Greatness Rises In each New Day" is meant to offer insights into how to live your best life. Read a chapter, or "Daily GRIND," a day to set your mind on the right path, or read it from cover to cover to let the message truly sink in. Read it once, or regularly revisit the parts that motivate you. The chapters are short, meant to be food for thought to provoke you to think about how to live your best life. The ideals of embracing the GRIND permeate each chapter, and although the message contained in each "Daily GRIND" is similar—the hope is that somewhere in the midst of the reflections, you find a passage that resonates with you and motivates you to great things.

No matter how you choose to use this book, remember the key concept:

Greatness awaits, but you have to go get it.

Live Your Dream

If you're ever going to get where you want to be, you have to know what you want. You need to spend some time seriously evaluating what it is you are striving for in your life and what it is you want to accomplish. Be specific and be bold.

If you're going to work your ass off for something, it better be something that you are fired up about. Take the time to sit down and truly think about the life that you want to live—professionally, socially, etc. Leave no aspect of your life unturned, and don't sell yourself short. Get rid of the "what ifs" and "that could never happen" and allow yourself to envision what your life would be like if you had everything you ever wanted. That being said—you have to be bold, but you also have to be realistic. If you envision yourself playing in the NBA, but are 5'2, forty years old, and have never played basketball before, then you're likely a little off the mark.

Think about every last detail as you envision your perfect life. It should excite you, and it should probably make you a little nervous too as you think about the work and dedication needed to get there. If the goals you set out for yourself are too easy to attain, then you are likely selling yourself short. But if they are bold and worthwhile, they'll require some serious work and effort on your part. You'll have to get out of your comfort zone and put yourself out there.

As you think about the future you desire, the more specific you are, the better. The next step is writing it down. Write down what it is you are hoping to achieve and look at it regularly. Post it on the fridge or on your bathroom mirror, or set it on the home screen of your cell phone. This may seem silly—but the constant reminder will keep you working toward your goals on those days when you lose sight of what you're working toward.

It's also helpful to share your goals with someone you trust. A little accountability can go a long way, and when you give voice to your vision and share it with someone in your life, you've upped the stakes—it's real now and there's no turning back. Ask that person to check in with you regularly to see what progress you're making. Be sure to choose someone you trust who will be honest with you. It's inevitable that you'll have moments where you waiver, and having someone to bring you back on track can be the difference between permanent derailment and a brief moment off course.

If you don't take the time to seriously lay out your goals and your ideal life, then you're less likely to get out of bed in the morning and start working toward making them a reality. If you have a general idea of what you want to do and to accomplish, that's a good start—but you need to get more specific. Once you have a true vision of what you're striving for, then it's easier to start the process of working toward it, and you'll have a better understanding of what you need to do to get there. If the vision of your goals is hazy, the work you do to get there will lack focus, and the end result will likely be short of what you are truly capable of if you approach it with a clear purpose. Be specific and be bold—this is your life, and you only get one shot at it.

Get Up and GRIND

- It's time to create your vision for what you want. Be specific. Write down your goals—professionally, socially, and in any other realm you'd like to focus on. Post them somewhere you will see them regularly.
- Identify who you can share your vision with. Make a concrete plan to meet with them to share your goals and ask if they will be your accountability partner.
- Identify what could get in the way of achieving these goals, and make a solid plan to overcome it.

Fill out the GRIND Goal Setting Sheet on the following pages if you would like a more specific format to assist you and to have something to reference in the future.

GRIND Goal Setting
"A goal is a dream with a deadline."
-Napoleon Hill

When setting goals you need to be specific, bold, and realistic. State your goals in the positive tense, choose goals that ignite a fire in you to work toward achieving them, and identify what you're going to do to start achieving them.

Take into consideration what you are currently capable of, and create a realistic timeline to achieve your goals. It can be helpful to set short, medium, and long-term goals. Short-term goals that are attainable yet challenging will help you gain confidence on your path toward reaching your long-term goals, mid-range goals keep you fired up for the big picture, and the long-term/lifetime goals are what we're ultimately working toward. Setting and achieving goals keeps you inspired and focused in the direction you want to go.

Short-Term Goals (1-6 Months)

My goals are:
- ➢
- ➢

My plan of action is:

Mid-Range Goals (6-12 Month)

My goals are:
- ➢
- ➢

My plan of action is:

Long-Term Goals (1-3 Years)

My goals are:
- ➢
- ➢

My plan of action is:

Lifetime Goals (what do you envision your life to look like in the grand scheme of things)

My goals are:
- ➢
- ➢

My plan of action is:

A little accountability can go a long way—find someone to share your goals with and hold you accountable.

I am going to share my goals with _____, and ask them to be my accountability partner.

When things don't go according to plan, I will remind myself why I started and what fires me up about my goals and vision.

My biggest motivations to achieve my goals are:

Virtuosity in Everyday Life

"Do the common uncommonly well." This concept, referred to as virtuosity, applies in all fields—from sports and the gym, to musicians, business owners, and even in regards to your relationships.

The theory of virtuosity in the gym is easy to see. You want to squat 500 pounds? Work on your air squat—that's right, no barbell, no weight—just you and the air. Master your footwork, your depth, keeping your core tight, the angle of your legs, keeping your torso upright, the gaze of your eyes. Work on perfecting all these minute details of the air squat, and it will pay dividends as you begin to add load. Try to squat 500 pounds without taking the time to master the air squat, and you will likely encounter some problems.

We see the concept of virtuosity applied in other areas as well, such as with musicians. The "Rule of 10,000" claims that in order to become a master at something, we must spend 10,000 hours of concentrated practice at it. Much of this practice is spent on perfecting the seemingly little things—without mastery of the basics, we cannot move on to greater things. Whether or not 10,000 is truly the magic number, the point remains the same—get to work on the small things, and don't overlook the time necessary to attain success and mastery.

The concept is simple, and yet the rewards are immense. Take the time, effort, and energy to continue to develop and master the seemingly "simple" things, and it will make you not only virtuous at those simple things, but will allow you to perform better at the more skilled and challenging things as well. How can we apply this idea of virtuosity to our everyday lives? Does the principle remain the same, that if we "do the common uncommonly well," we will see the reward in the greater things in our lives?

Each day we encounter so many "common" things that the tendency seems to be to breeze right over them, perhaps not giving them the attention they require. Virtuosity in everyday life may be as simple as starting with our daily interactions. How do you address and interact with the people you see daily? Is it common for you to barely acknowledge a loved one or a co-worker? What if you took the time to engage them every time you saw them—with eye contact, a smile, or a simple hello? Surely this "common" practice done better could lead to happier and more fulfilling interactions in the long term, leading to overall greater life satisfaction.

What about your job? Are there tedious tasks that you fail to give proper attention to? By shirking these smaller things, you could be hindering your long-term progress. When you are attentive to the seemingly small things, and take the time to handle them with your fullest effort and energies, it pays off in the long term. Although it may not seem like it at the time, the commitment to taking care of the details helps make the bigger picture run more smoothly and successfully.

When we set high and lofty goals, it's easy to become overwhelmed. The outcome may seem so far off in the distance that we don't know where to begin. Commit to the practice of virtuosity—begin working on the small things, trying to do them to the very best of your ability. As you gain competence in these things, the next step will naturally appear—and you'll be ready for it. As you continue on, one step at a time, working toward excellence in the "small" things, you are moving ever closer to your goal.

It's natural to make big plans and resolutions about how or what we are going to change in our lives. Although it's great and important to dream big, it's often the attentiveness to the smaller details that allows those dreams to become a reality. Amidst the chaos of life, be sure to take care of the little things.

If you are looking to make big changes in your life, consider being more attentive to the small details and the commonplace things that we often take for granted. Do the common uncommonly well.

Get Up and GRIND

> Do you regularly try to breeze over the "small things" in hopes of moving on to bigger things? Choose one seemingly small part of your day that nags at you and address it with your full energy. Make it a daily practice to address the little issues that arise with your full effort instead of putting them off.

You Are Who You Want to Become

EACH HALLOWEEN, KIDS ACROSS THE country ask themselves the question, "Who/what am I going to be for Halloween?" Will they be strolling the streets as a superhero, a princess, a monster, or an angel? They can be anything they want to be. That's one of the great things about this holiday—for that one day, you can choose to be whomever you want to be. But here's the great thing—we have that choice everyday. We can choose exactly who we want to be, and not just by putting on a costume for a day, but by truly becoming who we want to be. Yes, it may require a little more effort than heading out to the store and picking out a costume and some makeup, but ultimately we still decide who we become. It just requires consistency, time, and effort.

You want to be stronger and healthier? You have the power to decide to go to the gym, eat well, and make good decisions. You want to pursue that new job or promotion? Put in the work and the hours, and show that you are qualified, capable, and passionate about what you do. But there's a catch—unlike Halloween it's not just one day. We have to do these things everyday. Every day we have to work to become who we want to be. Your decisions and actions today lead to the person you will be tomorrow and the legacy you will leave behind. We can't let days slip away without working toward becoming a better version of ourselves.

Fear and being scared are other notions often associated with Halloween, and perhaps are also the things that are holding you back from being who you want to be. It's important to acknowledge your fear, but you do not need to accept it. Know and believe in what you are capable of, and do not let your fear of perhaps not being able to accomplish a task stop you. Acknowledge that you are afraid, but don't be stopped by that fear.

Are there ever times in your life where you let the fear of something stop you from working toward becoming the best version of yourself? Fear is a natural part of our existence. It's how we choose to handle that fear that matters. Will you let it get the best of you and never try, or will you recognize your fear and overcome it, allowing yourself to be a better you?

Pretending that we aren't afraid is of no use. Look your fear right in the eyes, and let it know that you will no longer accept its presence. You will work today and every day to become the best version of yourself possible, and become the person you want to be. Nothing will get in your way.

The rewards that we receive through consistent effort in bettering ourselves have the potential to last a lifetime. Forget about who you're going to pretend to be for one day, and continue to work on who you're going to genuinely be each day.

Get Up and GRIND

- If someone close to you was asked to describe you—what would they say? Write down what you would hope their answer would be, and evaluate if that is an accurate reflection of the life you live.
- What are you going to do today to help become the person you are trying to become?
- What fears hold you back from the work you to need to do to be your best self?

Get Your Shit Together

There's certainly a more eloquent way to state it, but perhaps not a way that conveys the message as directly as needed—get your shit together.

Stop making excuses, stop putting it off, stop thinking that you aren't capable. Start working toward your goals and creating a positive mindset that will enable you to get where you want to be.

There's not enough time and I don't have enough money. I don't have the resources. People will make fun of me if I go for this. I'm too tired to work on this. EXCUSES. Some of these may be true—to a point. But everyone only has twenty-four hours in a day and a finite amount of resources. Everyone gets run down and has struggles in their life, yet successful people find ways to overcome them. They don't allow these excuses to stop them from getting to work and putting in the necessary time and energy to achieve what they want. If you think you are the only one who has things going on in your life that could get in the way of your dreams and goals, you are gravely mistaken.

Determine what your strengths are and start putting them to work. Be honest about what your weaknesses are and begin attacking them. Don't get stuck in the trap of putting things off until tomorrow, or worse yet—next week, next month, or next year. This is your life, and it's happening right now. It doesn't start sometime in the future. You aren't magically going to wake up one day have it all together and know all the answers. You have to start the process now, even if you don't think you are ready for it yet. How else are you going to get there?

If everyone waited until they felt fully ready, nothing would ever get done—or at minimum it would take a lot longer. Sometimes we have to start working toward our vision before we feel completely prepared, because the reality is if we want to be our best selves and do great things, we have to get out of our comfort zones. Once you begin, you will learn lessons along the way, and gain the needed experience each step of the way. If you wait until you feel 100% ready, chances are you waited too long. Get started, take the first step. As you move along, you'll gain more confidence each step of the way while you work toward your desired end state.

If you wait until you have enough money, enough experience, or enough time—you're going to be waiting forever, because you'll always think you should have more before you start. But if you commit to starting where you are with what you currently have, you're already on the right path, and ahead of those who are waiting for the "perfect time." Attacking your goals wholeheartedly and going all in right now is infinitely better than putting it off and just thinking about it for the foreseeable future—and perhaps never even starting because you don't think the conditions are perfect.

So get your shit together and get going.

Get Up and GRIND

- What excuses are you making to stop you from getting started on working toward your goals?
- What strengths do you have that you can immediately put to work to get rolling on a new project or goal?
- What are you waiting for?! Get going.

Make Today the Best Day Ever

As we get older, it's easy to get in a rut and forget the natural excitement brought by different times of the year and each new day. Even as the seasons change each year, we can be uplifted by the change and newness of each season—natural times throughout the year to regroup and recharge. But perhaps the monotony of your job or social life leaves you feeling caught in an endless cycle of sameness, never appreciating the ebb and flow of the year or the beauty of individual days. You must find a way to rekindle that feeling of "newness" that you once experienced as a child as the seasons pass and time moves on around you, and embrace the possibilities that each new day brings. Commit to something new, appreciate the beauty that is around you, and let yourself be filled with childlike excitement. It's far too easy to let days, and even seasons, come and go without feeling the potential excitement that they bring.

Go into each day with the attitude that every day is better than the day before, thus making today THE BEST DAY EVER.

It's certainly true that we all have ups and downs, and every day may not seem like "the best day ever." But what if we took this idea and ran with it? Each day is a day to experience new things, meet new people, and learn new lessons. When we embrace this idea, it allows us to be open to greater possibilities that the world and those around us have to offer.

Life can be busy, and it can be hard to take the time to take care of ourselves—exercise, eat right, and commit to personal and professional growth. But if we carry with us this idea of newness and celebrating each day as if it is the best day of our entire lives—imagine the endless possibilities and boundless energy that we can cultivate. Instead of begrudgingly hitting the snooze button an extra time (or two) in the morning, try to remember that today brings with it the opportunity to work toward being a better version of yourself.

Whatever new habit you're trying to create—whether it is beginning a new exercise routine, eating better, or applying for a new job—the key is you have to start. This seems so obvious, and yet many people are so afraid to start that they continue to push it off again and again, and never even begin what they set out to do. Know that when you commit to taking the first step, the second will naturally follow.

If you're someone who already has a lot of healthy habits in place, how can you refocus and reenergize your commitments to ensure that you are making progress in the right direction? It's easy to get stuck doing what we've always done and thinking it's enough. But if what you are currently doing isn't leading you to your goals and bettering yourself, perhaps it's time to reevaluate what you could be doing differently. Don't get in the trap of getting stuck doing the same thing if it isn't working.

Wherever you're at physically and mentally, remember that it's never too late for a fresh start. Be invigorated by the energy that is around you, don't be hindered by a fear of starting something new, and strive to make today and every day the "best day ever."

Get Up and GRIND

> Do you allow yourself to embrace the possibilities of each new day, or do you get stuck in the monotony of the day to day? If you're stuck in a rut, what can you do to revitalize your current routine?
> What new practice can you start today to reenergize your daily routine?

Everything Happens for a Reason

EVERYTHING HAPPENS FOR A REASON—THE tricky thing is that we don't always see it when it's happening. Some people know from the time they are young what they want to do with their lives, while others go through life constantly wondering and seeking what it is they are meant to do.

Even if you are one of those people who have no idea where your destination may be—it's imperative to follow your heart and passion, and work relentlessly, despite not knowing what the outcome will be or where the road will take you.

It's easy when we're in the day-to-day shuffle to get carried away in the what-ifs and obsessed with the unknowns. But the reality is that we can never know what tomorrow will bring. You may think you have the perfect plan laid out, but the universe may have different plans for you. All we have is today—and all we can do is work diligently, doing things we love, to help prepare us for our unknown futures, while always remembering to appreciate the gifts and blessings of the present.

When you put your full effort and energies into all that you do, you are infinitely more likely to see success. Even when you don't know where the path is taking you, have faith in the process and your efforts.

Aristotle said, "We are what we repeatedly do. Excellence, then, is not an act but a habit." It's important then to create good habits that always lead us to bettering ourselves and the world around us. Even when we can not see what the future brings, if we work hard each day and implement habits of hard work, positivity, and selflessness, we are moving ever closer to a life of excellence. At the times when you feel lost or lacking direction, remember that things happen for a reason—if you are pursuing excellence you will end up right where you are supposed to be.

Many people fall into the trap of "paralysis by analysis"—they get so lost in analyzing the limitless possibilities of what "could" happen that they end up doing nothing. So afraid that they'll make the wrong decision, they make no decision at all (which, in reality, is in fact a decision—the decision to do nothing). We're not meant to stay in one place (at least metaphorically) and never learn or grow—you have to be willing to take chances and put yourself out there, even if you don't know what the outcome is going to be. Choosing to do nothing at all is delaying your progress. Do your research on the possibilities that are out there, ask those around you for their advice or support, and go with your gut. Follow your passion, work your ass off, and enjoy the journey.

Get Up and GRIND

- Reflect on an incident in your life that while at the time seemed daunting or unresolved, now you can look back on with clarity and see that it happened for a reason. Use this as a constant reminder that plans unfold in time, even if we can't see them while they're occurring.
- Identify one problem in your life that you are currently trying to make a decision on, but have been struggling to move forward on, perhaps due to a fear that you'll make the "wrong" decision. Make a list of all of the possible outcomes, good and bad, and choose which path you are going to take.

Remember that a decision toward progress made now with full gusto and effort is better than one never made at all.

Embrace Being Scrappy

THERE ARE MANY DIFFERENT WAYS to achieve success in life. This can be seen starting in school at a young age. Some students seemingly never have to open a textbook in their entire academic career and manage with flying colors. Then there are the kids making flashcards, coming up with ridiculous acronyms, and studying hours for exams in order to excel. At the end of the day people find success doing both of these different methods, but one just requires a little more effort and time. For those who it doesn't come naturally to, it would be easy to give up, but we all need to understand the value of consistent effort and its ultimate pay off.

The same idea can be seen in sports. In most sports there are "scrappy" players and "finesse" players. The finesse players make everything look easy and graceful, and often get much of the credit for beautiful plays and goals. The scrappy ones are the players battling it out in the corners, doing the dirty work—it may not be pretty, but it's got to be done. Scrappy players never necessarily make it look "easy"—you can always tell they are working. They work hard during competition and spend countless hours in the off-season preparing for the upcoming year. They love the grind, and you can find them spending extra time in the weight room, running stairs in a weight vest, and practicing extra hours to hone their skills. When the season rolls around they are always ready, despite the fact that they never have the look of a finesse player.

Whether it is in academics, athletics, or the business world, there's a great value in working hard. It's ok to be scrappy, and you should never be afraid to lay it all on the line. That extreme work ethic carries over into all aspects of your life, and it's only through extreme effort by which real success comes. In his book *Mastery* George Leonard says, "To take the master's journey, you have to practice diligently, striving to hone your skills, to attain new levels of competence."

In your current position, no matter what it may be, you need to remind yourself to "practice diligently" in all things even when it seems as if you are in a plateau. Try not to get down when something takes a little longer to learn, when it feels like you aren't making progress, or when it seems like everyone around you is seeing more success than you are.

GRIND: Greatness Rises In each New Day | 37

It's too easy to look at the person next to you and compare yourself to them and what they are capable of—but it's not about them and where they are. It's about you and pushing yourself harder than you thought you could, while still supporting those around you who are doing the same. We can fill our heads with negative thoughts as we look around in our lives and see people who it seemingly comes easy for. That person is stronger than I am, thinner than me, prettier than me, has more money than me—the list goes on and on. Stop comparing yourself to others. Get back to the grind, and embrace your own personal journey.

We are each blessed with many gifts and talents, and we can't forget to look around and take it all in. Appreciate the gifts you have, and try not to get so caught up in comparing yourself to others.

Whatever it is you're working on—no matter if its training for your first half marathon, preparing for a new job, or even formulating a more consistent gym or work routine—don't be afraid to put forth your full effort working toward becoming a better you. Just because things don't come easily, it doesn't mean they're not worth pursuing wholeheartedly. Far too often, we want things to be easy, but there's great value in the effort. Come to love the grind and embrace being the "scrappy" one. Know that if you continue to pursue excellence in all that you do, you will reap the rewards of your effort.

Get Up and GRIND

- Is there something in your life you are avoiding because it doesn't come easily to you or you aren't good at it? If you can identify something you're avoiding due to the fear of how long it will take you to complete the task, how can you overcome your aversion to it and put in the work necessary to overcome it? Come up with a plan, and get to work.
- Would you characterize yourself as being "scrappy?" How can you put the value of being scrappy to work in your life?

A Universal Resolution

PEOPLE ARE CONSTANTLY MAKING RESOLUTIONS and goals for their lives. In fact, each New Year it seems like everywhere you turn someone is resolving to give something up, do something more, or change something major. This isn't a bad thing, in fact quite the opposite. This shared cultural desire we see during that time of year to better ourselves, our lives, and those around us should be harnessed to do just that—make the world a better place! Perhaps this seems overly simplistic, but seriously consider what change, great or small, you can do to make your life and the lives of those around you better (and you don't even have to wait until the New Year). It doesn't have to be big—even the smallest actions and behaviors can have a ripple effect. Charles Duhigg, in *The Power of Habit,* speaks about how we each have "keystone habits." These are habits that when changed cause a ripple effect and change other habits that we have. For example, research shows that exercise is one of these keystone habits—when one commits to exercising, they have a tendency to eat better, be more productive at work, show more patience, and feel less stress.

Take a serious look at your life and see if you can identify one or two keystone habits that you can improve upon, which in turn will help to make your life as a whole better. It's amazing how oftentimes when we choose to enhance one part of our life, we see positive and desirable benefits in other areas.

Once you've taken the time to identify these personal habits and resolutions consider one more resolution. This resolution is for all people, no matter the time of year or what other keystone habits they are working on. It is, *"Surround yourself with positive people, and be one of those positive people for others."* This seemingly simple resolution can change your life, and likely make keeping any other resolutions you make easier. It's amazing what a good support system can do, not only in helping you achieve your goals, but also in making your life more satisfying as a whole.

When people around you believe in you and support your aspirations, everything seems to be more attainable. Conversely, if you surround yourself with negative people, it's a lot harder to reach your goals and enjoy life's daily blessings while they are trying to tear you down. Relationships are what make life meaningful, fun, and ultimately worth living—fill your life with people who care about you and encourage you to be your best self.

The second part of this universal resolution is just as important, perhaps more so: be a positive person for others, enhancing the communities you are part of and the many lives that you touch. Positivity is infectious, and there's little doubt that by being a beacon of positivity for others it will be returned to you when you most need it. It's unrealistic to think that problems don't happen and every day is perfect, but when we consistently seek the best in situations, we begin to see more and more good around us.

As you go about each day, approach it with a positive attitude, surround yourself with positive and life giving people, and become the best version of yourself.

Get Up and GRIND

- What is one keystone habit you can create within the next week to have a positive butterfly effect throughout your life? Commit to doing the habit every day for the next 10 days.
- Identify the top five people you interact with on a daily basis—are they positive people who act as inspiring influences to you? Do they support you as you work toward your hopes and dreams? If yes—great, take some time to thank them for their positive impact on your life. If not, where can you find others who will support and motivate you to become your best self?
- Do you act as a role model of positivity and support to those around you? Recommit to being a true, loyal, and supportive influence on the lives of those you encounter.

I Just Got Better

Over the door of the weight room of a prestigious college with a successful athletic program, there's a sign that states, "I Just Got Better." Each day as athletes leave the weight room after their rigorous training sessions they slap that sign. It doesn't matter if they're exhausted from practice, lifting, sprints, or whatever other crazy training session their strength coach put them through that day—they lift their tired arms and hit that sign. They learned early on in their collegiate athletic careers that hitting the sign was important—and it was a constant reminder that working hard day in and day out did, in fact, make them better. They had to put in a consistent effort, and it wasn't easy—but they were a little bit better every time they left the weight room.

This lesson holds true in the workplace as well. We live in a society where often times we want everything all at once—but life doesn't work like that. We need to put in the work each day, doing the little things over and over again—

the right way—before we notice any real progress. And yet despite the fact that sometimes it seems as if we're not moving forward…we, in fact, get better every day if we press on, putting in the work, consistently attacking challenges, and overcoming life's little obstacles.

It seems like everyone always has a laundry list of things that they want to accomplish. Perhaps right before the summer season, they have the sudden realization that the six-pack and perfect beach body they had hoped to have in time for the summer isn't quite "ready" yet. So they hit the gym and commit to dialing in their diet. It goes well for a few days, hey maybe even a few weeks. But then… "Wait a second, I've been doing this for two whole weeks and I don't have a six-pack yet—what's the deal? I haven't gotten any better." And so they stop going to the gym, convinced their efforts aren't working. It's times like these that we have to go back to that lesson learned in the weight room—you did just get better. A little better everyday, but things take time. We want things now, but success and mastery come from the consistent effort—not for a day or a week or a month, but every day over time.

If you feel like you get stuck in a rut, try to recruit a friend to get you back on track and help motivate you. If you aren't seeing the results you want, in any aspect of your life, despite a consistent effort over time, don't be afraid to switch it up. Perhaps you have a friend who you know has experienced success in the area you are hoping to get better at—ask them what they do and glean any information or advice you can from them. Find a community that will push and encourage you, even during those periods where you struggle to get motivated. This can be the difference between giving up on your efforts, and breaking through a plateau, stronger and more successful than ever.

Whatever it is you're striving for, remember the real reasons why you are reaching for that goal. We all want to live a better, healthier, and more energized and fulfilled life. Enjoy the process. Worry less about the little setbacks along the way, and think more about all the little steps you have made in the right direction. Does the life you live leave you feeling strong and empowered? Do you take pride in your efforts—knowing that you put your best effort forward and pushed on even when it was challenging? Are you a positive influence to those around you? Does what you are reaching for make you truly happy? Hopefully the answer to these questions is yes, even if you haven't quite reached your goal yet. Be consistent and patient, confident that when you put your best effort forth worthwhile results will follow.

At the end of the day we all want to be the best versions of ourselves. Better spouses, parents, siblings, friends, and co-workers. Let your endeavors energize and excite you—have faith that when you work hard you are getting better each and every day. Better physically, better mentally, and all in all, a better version of yourself.

Get Up and GRIND

> What is something you have been working on, but haven't yet reaped the rewards of your work? Is the effort you are putting forth well guided, or does it need to be reevaluated and refocused? Enlist a friend to help you reach this goal, and recommit to your best effort each day to get there, even if it doesn't happen overnight.

Sisu—Strength in Adversity

EARLY MORNINGS, LONG DAYS, LATE nights… Business commitments, family commitments, personal commitments… Time constraints, money constraints, health constraints… Yes, life can be hard. We all deal with a host of issues on a daily basis, and it's easy for even the most levelheaded person to get overwhelmed. But this is life—and instead of dreading the day-to-day grind, we're called to find ways to embrace, overcome, and ENJOY each moment we have here—even if sometimes it seems that life can overwhelm us.

The Finnish culture has a word, "sisu," that roughly translates to "strength of will, determination, perseverance, and acting rationally in the face of adversity." It is not that one with the quality of sisu does not experience failure, but it is rather that they press on, despite setbacks or odds that are seemingly not in their favor. Sisu means having guts. We can strive for sisu everywhere—in the gym, at work, at school, and in life as a whole.

Life requires all of us to have a certain level of sisu when things get tough, which they inevitably will. The concept of sisu is easy to see played out in the gym. There are days you don't want to train—so sore or tired that the thought of even going to the gym seems exhausting. Or maybe it's a hot, sunny day and the beach is calling your name—you feel like there's simply no way to get your workout in on a day as beautiful as this! But we must remember sisu—the concept bringing us back to reality, reminding us that we must not only persevere, but thrive. Other days getting to the gym is easy, but once there, while in the midst of your training session, it all seems too hard. It's too heavy, you're too slow, the miles seem endless. Sisu. Have guts, press on.

The concept of sisu is easy to see in the gym or on the playing field when athletes work through tough days and tackle their workouts with determination, blood, sweat, and tears. But there are certain people who, whether they know it or not, live this ideal out in all aspects of their lives and inspire us with their remarkable ability to not only overcome adversity, but show amazing strength and goodness throughout their struggles. They remind us that most of the problems we deal with are small, and that no matter how big the struggle, we can be courageous and positive in the face of even the worst situations.

Parents who have lost their children to war, disease, or addiction—but fight on anyway and continue to try to make the world around them a better place. Children who grow up in broken homes with little resources, but still manage to earn an education and become successful. The list goes on and on. We all face struggles in life, but those who live a life of "sisu" show strength, determination, will and purpose despite this adversity. Despite their struggles, they live their life fully and passionately, help others in need and press on relentlessly. They show us their unconquerable spirit and take nothing for granted.

When you get overwhelmed, and life seems to be too tough, keep things in perspective and remember the idea of sisu—be strong, press on, and make your corner of the world a better place.

Get Up and GRIND

- Think of someone you know who lives out the concept of "sisu" through their perseverance and determination in the face of adversity. Reflect on what it is about this person that allows them to overcome obstacles in their life, and work to emulate that in your own life.
- What adversities have you faced in your own life, or are you currently facing? How did you, or can you, apply the theory of sisu to these struggles?

Make Tomorrow Your Lucky Day

Do you believe in luck? The word luck elicits different images and emotions in people. Perhaps you think of winning the lottery, landing a great job, being in a great relationship, or maybe a leprechaun sitting with a pot of gold at the end of the rainbow ready to give you your hearts desires. Maybe you consider yourself to be someone with great luck, or on the contrary, someone with horrible luck—perhaps lingering years after breaking a mirror or stepping on a crack as a child.

It seems like there is a great commonality in what "successful" people view as luck. Benjamin Franklin said, "Diligence is the mother of good luck." The film producer Samuel Goldwyn took a similar outlook, saying, "The harder I work the luckier I get." Serena Williams, winner of multiple gold medals at the Olympics, said about her success, "Luck has nothing to do with it, because I have spent many, many hours, countless hours, on the court, working for my one moment in time, not knowing when it would come."

Whether they are successful in politics, film, athletics, business, or other endeavors, the common link is hard work. Yes, being in the right place at the right time helps—but how do you think these people got there? Constantly, relentlessly working toward their goal—even if they were uncertain when the time would arise when all that hard work would be tested. That's the thing about success—rarely does it come overnight. It's countless hours spent working on the details. Over and over again. Never settling for less than perfect, even when perfect seems far away or unattainable. It's easy to watch professional athletes make the buzzer beater shot and call it lucky. Or to watch a musician beautifully and elegantly play a piece and chalk it up to "natural ability." But ask those people what it took to get there and you would likely see a deeper story—one involving incalculable hours working toward perfecting their craft, and undoubtedly many sacrifices made along the way.

Many believe that everything happens for a reason, and we end up right where we're supposed to be, and perhaps being lucky plays into that. But when you work hard in pursuing what you desire, you are more likely to end up right where you're supposed to be. Don't let the hands of fate dictate what you do, and more importantly don't use bad luck or lack of time as an excuse to not pursue what you desire. Prioritize what's important to you, and involve those you love in your pursuits.

Don't be one of those people who make excuses, or say things like, "I would be in shape/strong/fit/ripped if I worked out and ate better." Yes, yes you would. If you really believe that, then act on it! If being fit and healthy is important to you, then don't count on luck to get you where you want to be. If you want a promotion at your job, work for it—show up early, stay late and produce great work. Take the lessons learned from successful people and put them into use—work toward what you want!

Remember that luck benefits those who consistently work hard, day in and day out, even when they're having a bad day, or are momentarily lacking motivation. No matter what your hopes and goals are, put in the work daily, surround yourself with people who believe in you and motivate you, and believe that the work that you do today may make tomorrow your lucky day!

Get Up and GRIND

> Have you ever used the excuse of bad luck to explain your lack of success or progress toward something? What habits can you create to alter your mindset to one where you take full credit for your own success or failure?

Don't Wish It Away

IN WINTER, PEOPLE YEARN FOR summer. In the afternoons, people can't wait for their workday to be over. On Mondays, people are already counting down until Friday.

But do you really want to wish away seasons, afternoons, or four out of seven days waiting for the weekend? Seek to find enjoyment and be more appreciative every day. Each day is a gift and an opportunity. An opportunity to build relationships, experience life's small moments of wonder, and to become a better version of yourself.

Not everyone is lucky enough to enjoy the beauty that each day brings. Work to rekindle in yourself a commitment to appreciate your own life and gifts. Appreciate the gift of life by taking care of your body. Live a life of passion and selflessness. Move, sweat, play, and enjoy the gift of human movement and ability. Each day when you wake up realize that, although there may be ups and downs, ultimately the days are meant to be cherished and lived with passion and vigor.

Don't wish away Mondays—don't wait until Friday afternoon to enjoy your life. Wake up each morning and cherish the day—create a life worth living and live it up.

It's important to take time to be aware of the many gifts that we have in our lives and the blessings that each day brings. Far too often we let days slip by without taking the time to be grateful for what we have. The unfortunate reality is that sometimes it takes us losing something before we truly appreciate it.

Make a concentrated effort to take the time to appreciate the gifts that you have that you often overlook. Change your mindset from "I have to" into "I get to." It's amazing what this small change in your way of thinking can do. This is your life; take the time to enjoy the daily gifts and blessings. It's easy to let days, months, even years go by without stopping to appreciate what we have. Your health, your job, your family—don't take these things for granted. What are the things in your life that happen every day that you sometimes fail to appreciate? Take a moment to savor these little blessings.

Take this attitude of gratitude and "I get to do it" into all parts of your daily routine, and you may be pleasantly surprised with how much more productive and fun it is.

If you are healthy and well, embrace the fact that you are capable of working out. Fuel your body with the right foods and exercise regularly. There are many people out there riddled with injuries and poor health who yearn for the chance to train, or even just enjoy being able to get around easily.

Instead of begrudgingly heading to your job, be grateful if you have a job that supports you and your family. Instead of going about your daily tasks with a negative attitude, embrace the challenge to attack these tasks and do them well.

Wake up each day with an indomitable spirit, an attitude of gratitude, and a desire to make the day meaningful. Coach John Wooden is quoted as saying that we should "make each day our masterpiece." If today was the only day you had—what would you do with it? Surely you wouldn't let it slip away without taking a moment to look around at the gifts you've received. What can you do today to make a positive impact in the world and to those around you? Don't wait for tomorrow—appreciate today, go all in, and make it your masterpiece.

Get Up and GRIND

- Make a list of things in your life that you take for granted, but ultimately truly appreciate. Check back on this list regularly and find new ways to show appreciation for the daily gifts you have.
- Go all in with your life. Make today, and every day, your masterpiece.

Transformative Love

HAVING FRUITFUL AND LIFE GIVING relationships is critical to living your best life. Just like being attentive to your diet and exercise are integral parts of living a healthy life, it's just as important to take care of your personal relationships and your emotional wellbeing.

Although often when we hear the word love we think of romantic love, it's important to reflect on the power of love as a whole, and the very real notion that love can and should make you and those around you better, and reveal a more beautiful world and life.

Paulo Coelho has a quote that speaks to this concept: "When we love, we always strive to become better than we are. When we strive to become better than we are, everything around us becomes better too." The question you need to ask of yourself is: do the people and things in your life you claim to love make you better, and therefore transform the world around you into a better place as well? You are capable every day in partaking in loving relationships that transform the world into a better place. The love you create, both by accepting and offering it to others, can illuminate the world. So too you are capable of putting such love into your work and daily responsibilities that the world is better simply by your being, and you lovingly offering yourself to the world.

Strive to have relationships in your life that are built on a love that transforms, a love that enhances. This is true for all of your relationships, not just with your significant other, but also with your friends, your co-workers, your family, and those you regularly encounter. Have you surrounded yourself with people who help make you better than you are? Do you act to lovingly make those in your life better? If we are to believe Coelho, then if you answered yes to these questions, everything around you will become better too. Conversely, if you find yourself in relationships that leave you feeling neglected, disempowered, useless, or unloved—it is perhaps time to reevaluate who you associate with. You are worthy of great love, love that betters you and the world. Don't settle for anything less than this!

In addition to partaking in genuinely loving relationships, we can also bring love into our daily actions. If you can find passion in your daily routine, and allow your life's work to contribute to the betterment of the human condition—you are without a doubt helping to make the world a better place. Create a life that allows you to do what you love every day and make those around you better through your actions. This could, in fact, be our greatest calling—making those around us better through our love and actions.

Find a community who truly pushes you and supports you in becoming the best version of yourself. Find those people who make you feel alive and capable of greatness—because you are.

Seek, offer, and accept relationships and a life that embody love in its truest sense—a love that makes you and everything around you better.

Get Up and GRIND

- Do you approach your life, relationships, and work with love?
- As you read this chapter, did you identify with the idea of living a life that you love and that also transforms the world into a better place to be? If not—what can you do to make this your reality?

Passionately Pursue Your Goals

It is of critical importance to set goals that you are passionate about, and evaluate what it takes to attain them. Be so fired up about your goals that you are willing to do whatever it takes to accomplish those goals, even if it means making sacrifices in the short term, and working hard every single day.

You can set goals based on your career, relationships, fitness, or any other area of your life. No matter what it is you are reaching for, there are some commonalities that will make it easier for you to work toward making your goals a reality.

Perhaps the most important aspect of a goal is that it is something that, when you think about it, ignites a passion within you. Just the thought of attaining it leaves you inspired, motivated, and ready to do whatever it takes to get you there. Sometimes when others look at someone who is single-mindedly pursuing a goal, they view them as crazy. Others may knock you down or try to deter you from working toward and reaching your goal, but if it is something you truly desire, nothing will stop you.

Once you've identified your goal, the next key to success is good old-fashioned hard work. This seems so obvious—but it's surprising how many people say they want something yet aren't willing to put in the time, and do the work to attain it. You'd like to run a marathon? Awesome—are you willing to put in the miles, dial in your nutrition and sleep, and make sacrifices in other areas of your life? Maybe you're seeking new employment or a promotion. Are you willing to work long hours, go the extra mile and put yourself out there? It takes more than talking about something to achieve it—yet when push comes to shove, too many people let their dreams go because they aren't willing to go all in. Be fearless, lay it on the line, and don't let the fear of failure stop you from putting in the necessary work required for success.

Arguably, the most important part of realizing your goals is having a rock-solid support system. It could be your friends, a significant other, your family, or your team—but you need people around you who support you and believe in you. When you are working toward your goals you'll undoubtedly come up against obstacles and self-doubt, but having a good support system helps you work through this and keep your eye on the prize. Don't be mistaken and think that you have to go it alone. Having a group of people around you who believe in you could likely be the difference between reaching your goal and coming up short.

Be passionate, work hard, and surround yourself with positive people. Be willing to go the extra mile and do what others aren't willing to do to move ever closer to making your dream a reality. If and when you do reach your goal, don't forget to reflect back on where you've come from, celebrate with those who were part of the journey, and cheers to your success!

Get Up and GRIND

- Review the goals that you wrote earlier. Assess your progress and update the goals if necessary—make sure the goals you wrote still fire you up and ignite a passion within you to work toward them.
- Set a follow-up meeting with your accountability partner and discuss your progress. Be honest with them about what is going well and where you've fallen short.
- Since setting your initial goals, what victories have you had? Take some time to celebrate the progress you have had, and let it fuel you as you continue working toward your goals.

Big Commit

LIFE IS EASIER WHEN YOU commit. When you have a halfway approach to your life—in your work, your education, your training, your relationships—plan on only having a life that is half-way fulfilled. The problem is that fully committing can be extremely scary. When it comes to big decisions people often hesitate. Although it's important to weigh the consequences of our decisions, once you've made up your mind on something, you have to GO ALL IN. You can't let the fear of what could possibly go wrong stop you from pursuing what you desire wholeheartedly.

In sports, hesitation can cost games. It's those players who aren't afraid to lay it on the line who win games and who we remember. They don't hesitate to lay out to block a shot or take the buzzer beater shot. They know that if they hesitate even a fraction of a second—if they fail to go all in—the game could be lost.

But how do these great players gain the confidence to go all in and lay it all on the line? They practice their asses off. They work incessantly in the gym, in training, and in studying their opponent, so that when the game is on the line, their instinct takes over. They don't wait until the season is on the line to commit. They set themselves up for success months, and sometimes years, before, in the off-season, showing up and grinding every day. People want the fame and glory that goes along with success, but often forget about the level of commitment it takes to get there.

There are no shortcuts. There's no magic pill for success, and those at the top would tell you they wouldn't want one. There's something about knowing that you've worked your ass off in order to achieve what you have that makes it all that much sweeter. It's the mishaps and struggles along the way that make the taste of victory that much better and more fulfilling. If you want something bad enough, you better be willing to work for it.

Although the risk may be bigger, when we fully commit to things, the rewards are also far greater. If you never apply to your dream job, ask out your crush, try out for the team, or audition for the starring role—you're never going to get it. The fact seems so obvious, and yet is so often forgotten or overlooked.

But what if you do decide to go all in and it doesn't work out—what happens then? Shame, grief, and self-doubt take over, and you spend the rest of your life living in a pool of your own tears and misery. Kidding. You learn from your mistakes, figure out what you need to do to attain success, and recommit to the GRIND. Find people who have attained what you want and ask them for advice. Learn more, practice more, commit more. One failed attempt doesn't make you a failure, unless you let that be the end of the road. It's a step on the journey, but you have to keep marching forward. Commit big, go all in, and never stop the process of working toward what you desire.

Get Up and GRIND

➤ Do you commit to what you want, or do you let fear stop you from going all in?
➤ Choose one project or goal that you are currently pursuing and evaluate if you are fully committing to it. If not, what are you afraid of? Allow yourself to imagine the best-case AND worse-case scenarios that could happen regarding this goal. Recognize that, in most cases, even if the worst-case scenario comes to fruition, it would not make your work a total failure, whereas the commitment to go all in allows for more growth and long-term success.

Just Keep Moving

INERTIA. ONCE YOU START MOVING, you're likely going to keep moving in the same direction. This leads us back to the main concept of this book—get up, show up, and GRIND. You have to start! For whatever reason starting something new is typically the hardest part for people. But once you have that routine, the power of habit takes over and the wheels of progress are in motion.

Successful people know how important the mental side of success is. In sport, athletes train not only their bodies but their minds—when their bodies are screaming out in exhaustion telling them to stop, it's the strength of the mind that allows them to continue charging forward. But when the mind has decided that it is too tired to go on, the body readily succumbs to fatigue and exhaustion.

Learn how to create positive mantras in your head to reinforce the behavior you desire. Mantras should be short and concise, able to be repeated over and over until the positive message sinks in. "Strong and Confident," "Just Keep Moving," and "Lean and Drive" are a few examples of mantras that can keep you moving in the right direction. It's best to phrase things in the positive if you want positive results. If your mantra is "Don't Stop, Don't Stop, Don't Stop," at some point your mind and body are going to block out the "don't" and just hear the "stop"—which is the opposite of what we're hoping to achieve.

The voices in our head can be loud, therefore it's critical to make sure that they are leading us in the right direction. You have to fight the demons inside your mind and let them know who is in charge. When a negative thought comes into your mind, quickly replace it with a more positive one that will help your cause. Everyone has demons in their head at certain points—so it's important to be able to quiet them when they rear their ugly heads.

One such demon that many people experience is imposter or fraud syndrome. Imposter syndrome happens to even the most successful people, and occurs when an individual, despite their success, has a constant fear that they are going to be "found out," or exposed as a fraud. The demons inside their head tell them that they are not good enough or smart enough to have the success that they have achieved, and they constantly worry that someone is going to reveal them as a fake or phony. Although this occurs at different levels, it's safe to say that at some point we've all felt like this. We've doubted ourselves and our abilities, despite the fact that we have attained some level of success.

How do we combat this self-doubt? First, you have to acknowledge that it's there—shoving it to the back of your mind only means that it will someday creep its way back into the forefront of your thoughts and wreak havoc again. Secondly—know that if you've put in the work, you are right where you are supposed to be. We all have self-doubt, but if you have properly prepared for the position that you are in, you are capable of greatness within that position. Thirdly—always keep learning and working to be better. This doesn't mean becoming obsessive, or letting a perfectionist mindset paralyze you, but it does mean committing to being the best at whatever you set out to do. If you acknowledge your doubts, recognize the work you've put in to get where you are, and commit to the lifelong process of bettering yourself—you have no reason to feel like an imposter. Work hard to get where you want to be, and have pride in your accomplishments.

Get Up and GRIND

- Create a personal mantra that will enable you to keep moving in the right direction when the voices of self-doubt come into your head. Be sure that it is concise and set in the positive, and begin the practice of repeating it to yourself often in your mind.
- Have you ever felt like you are an imposter and are going to be "found out" as a fraud? If so, identify the work you have done to get where you are, and replace those doubts with a positive self-affirmation and belief in self.

Fear Not

Everybody worries about life—their job, their health, their relationships, how they compare to others—the list goes on and on. But what is the point of all of this worry? It's been said many times that often the fear of failure is worse than failure itself, and there's certainly some validity to this statement.

So many people spend so much time worrying about the worst-case scenario that they end up living their lives in a constant state of worry rather than enjoying the present moment and the goodness that is around them. It's important to plan for the future and be aware of possible outcomes, both positive and negative, to your endeavors. But we can't be consumed by playing out every worst-case scenario over and over in our head and dwelling over it incessantly.

The reality is that most of what we waste our energy fearing probably is never going to happen, so why waste our time fearing it? Not to mention that, although you may like to, you can't control everything. It's important to focus on what you can control—your effort and your response to things.

You can control your effort. You may not know what's coming, but there's a certain confidence and peace of mind that can be attained when you know you've given it your all. If you've put in the work, when self-doubt and fear rear their head, you can counter them by remembering all the work you've put in to get where you are. If in the end that isn't enough—at least you will have no doubts about your effort.

You can also control how you respond to whatever life brings your way, and it's not always going to go like you planned. When it doesn't, you have to find ways to understand and improve upon the situation. Problem solve, don't panic. Fear and a sense of panic can lead to being paralyzed into inaction, which can lead to giving up on your goals unnecessarily.

If you still find yourself obsessively worrying about what failures could happen, and what could go wrong, one tactic to combat this is to allow yourself to truly think about what would happen if the worst-case scenario actually played out. Not in a fruitless way that leads to panic, but in a practical way. What if you asked out the girl and she said no? What if you applied for the job and didn't get it, or you lost the job you currently have because you proposed an idea management didn't like? What if you try out for a team and don't make it, or audition for a play and don't get the role? Chances are the worst-case scenario you are so worried about is not that horrible, and if it did happen you would surely find a way to overcome it. In fact, the regret you would have from not even trying because you are too scared is likely far worse than the failure of putting yourself out there and not finding immediate success. Because of course one failure doesn't make YOU a failure—it's just a step on the journey. We move on, we problem solve and get back to work—but we don't get paralyzed by panic and fear. So it didn't work out like you thought it was going to—what's next? Assess what worked and what didn't, and create a plan to reach the goals you desire. Get your mindset right, and set forth on the path of attacking your goals relentlessly.

Get Up and GRIND

➤ What are the things you currently spend the most time worrying about? Write them down and spend a few minutes thinking about the true "worst-case scenario" of each. Don't allow this to become a depressing, fruitless reflection—but instead try to realize that most of what you spend time worrying about is just wasting your time and energy. Make note of what you can and can't control, and cross things off the "worry list" that you have no control over, that aren't really a big deal, or in reality are probably never going to happen. With the items left on the list after this, make a plan to address your worry in a practical way, so that you can clear your mind from the consuming thoughts you have about them. Recognize that you cannot control everything, and that it's not worth wasting your time and energy on those things that you cannot control.

Haters Gonna Hate

YOU LIVE THE GRIND. You get up, show up, and work hard for what you want. Guess what—there are going to be plenty of people in your path who mock you and try to bring you down. It's an unfortunate reality, and for people who are earnestly seeking out their best self, it can be hard to understand. Why would someone try to knock you down when you are only trying to become the best version of yourself? There are countless reasons, but at the end of the day you have to be able to take it with a grain of salt. If you're truly working to make yourself and the world around you better, then you can't let the negativity of others wear on you.

It's healthy to care what other people think about you, to a point. But you can't be consumed by it, and you have to always consider the source. It's a hard reality to learn that not everyone will be pleased when you find success and happiness, and many will throw doubt and negativity at you as you try to get there.

It can be intimidating for people when they see someone wholeheartedly pursuing their dreams, especially if they are not doing it themselves. Perhaps they are jealous or unhappy with their own lives, so they feel the need to put you and your efforts down. Maybe they think your hopes and dreams are naïve, and make fun of you by calling your efforts fruitless or foolhardy. Let them. When people see someone working relentlessly toward their goal, they either get on board and support them, or try to knock them down. Those who try to knock you down aren't worth your time and effort. Sadly, some people have succumbed to a negative and pessimistic outlook on life, so stuck in their own unfulfilling realities that they try to bring you down with them. They aren't happy or successful—so they don't want you to be.

Although it's ok to try to get these people on board with you and see your side of things, it's not worth your time or energy to worry about it if they don't come around. Take the high road, be pleasant, and continue doggedly working toward your goals.

Truly successful people help build others up, not tear them down. Just as there are going to be people who try to get in the way of the pursuit of your goals, there will also be plenty who support you and believe in what you're fighting for. These are the people who deserve your energy, not the haters. For those who attain success through hard work and determination, they rarely worry or get jealous of others who are striving to do the same. They know the effort it takes to get to the top, and are far more likely to support you than tell you your aspirations are stupid and not worth fighting for.

As you work toward your goals, seek out help and guidance from those who have attained success. Although some may not be willing to assist you, chances are you will find plenty of people who are willing to offer advice and support if you are willing to put yourself out there and ask. Be open to constructive criticism—this is far different and more helpful than the negative input given to you by the haters. Constructive criticism is meant to lead us toward bettering what we are doing, whereas the pessimistic noise from the haters is only used to discourage us from putting in the necessary work needed to achieve our goals. Know the difference, and be grateful to those people who give you thoughtful feedback on what you are working on—even though sometimes it can be tough to hear.

As you work toward greatness, no matter the endeavor, there are going to be plenty of lessons you'll need to learn along the way. Allow yourself to learn from the successes and failures of others, and be open to feedback from those who are truly trying to help you. The sooner you realize that you don't know everything and that you don't have to go it alone, the faster you'll get to your goal.

Get Up and GRIND

- What, if any, haters have you encountered? What was your response to them, and more importantly did you allow their negativity to affect you? If so, what are some concrete strategies you can employ to ensure you don't allow them to deter you from your goals?
- Who are some people you can reach out to as you seek out a goal?
- Who are the experts in your field that you look up to? What lessons can you learn from them?

Come Back

The journey to greatness and achieving your goals isn't easy, and no one ever claimed it would be. Yes, the key is consistently showing up and working hard. But the truth is, at some point most people will probably falter, get off track, and lose sight of what they're working for. It's hard to work day after day toward something, knowing that the end result may still be far in the distance. There's a lot of sacrifice that goes into reaching your goals, and sometimes it can get to be too much. So we wander off, we get distracted, and our work ethic drops off.

But if you ever fall off track, remember that doesn't have to mean that your vision is gone forever. There are lots of reasons we can get distracted from our goals. Perhaps you're feeling burned out, overwhelmed, like you're not making the progress you had hoped for, or helpless. Maybe other parts of your life—your relationships, your work, etc. have taken so much of your time and energy that you had to put working on your goal on the back burner. All of this is understandable, but it doesn't have to be the end of the line.

Assess why it is you fell off your journey—and if you decide it's still something you're passionate about, make a plan to recommit to your pursuits. When you wander off, especially if it's for an extended period of time, it can often be intimidating to return to your endeavors—but know that taking the first step back will likely be the hardest part. But if it's worth it, it must be done.

In an ideal world, there would be no obstacles in our path to making our dreams our reality, but we all know that's not the way that life works. There will be distractions, obstacles, and hiccups along the way. Anticipate it and forge the fortitude needed to overcome it. Remember, too that the obstacles can be from external sources, but often they are unnecessarily self-imposed.

Perhaps some of the most common self-imposed hurdles on the path to achieving your goals are self-doubt and giving up too soon, which often go hand in hand. Your goals should be big, so unless you've created a goal that is too small for what you are capable of, it will take time to achieve. In the early stages, it's easy to get excited about working toward it—the long hours and sacrifices all seem worth it.

But as time goes on and the hours add up, it's easy to feel discouraged if you haven't reached your goal, especially if you don't feel like you are getting any closer to attaining it. This is usually when self-doubt starts to creep in. It taunts you silently in your mind in a voice that no one else can hear, but sounds deafening to you. Who are you to have success? You're not worthy of it. Why are you bothering with this? It's not going to work anyway. Do you really think you are capable of this? You should probably stop and save yourself the embarrassment of failure.

The good thing is that you ultimately have control over these voices and doubts in your head. It's normal to have them, but you must be proactive in combating them. Do not let them reside in your head and take root. Replace these negative thoughts with positive ones, and stay on track. Be courageous in the face of doubt, and have faith in yourself and your abilities. Those who attain success rarely get there without experiencing some doubt or obstacles along the way—the path to the top is rarely a straight one.

When you feel like you are stuck in a rut and doubt starts to wash over you, remember why you set out on your goal. Find new inspiration and commitment—prove the voices in your head wrong. When people feel like they are stuck in a plateau for too long, they often give up. But those who attain mastery and success continue on during these times, and inevitably eventually break through the plateau, and come out stronger and closer to what they set out to do.

If you get off track, no matter the reason, remember that you are only ever one decision away from getting back on the path to where you want to be. Don't let one mistake or a temporary break in your dedication be the end of your resolve. Get back to the GRIND, and work for what you desire.

Get Up and GRIND

> ➤ What setbacks have cropped up on your journey? Have you let them get in the way of achieving your goals? If so, what can you do to get back on track? Make a plan and take the first step.

> ➤ Have you placed any self-imposed restraints upon yourself? What can you do to knock them down and overcome them?

Choose To Be Happy, Choose To Be You

ONE OF THE MOST IMPORTANT things to remember, and yet the easiest to forget, is that we get to choose our inner-most thoughts and how we respond to what's going on around us. No matter what anyone says or does, ultimately you get to decide your thoughts and reactions to the outside world.

Clearly, this is often easier said than done—it is human nature to be impacted by what others say and think about us. But we have to remember that although everyone is entitled to their opinions, only you can decide who you truly are and determine your belief system. That doesn't mean that everyone is going to like it, but at least you know that you are being your authentic self.

When you live your life constantly worrying about what others think about you and allow that to change who you are and deviate from being your true self, you are doing not only yourself, but the world, a disservice. The world needs you, not someone imitating others or conforming to what they think they are supposed to do or be.

Each of us has our own unique personality and gifts, and if we stifle those in order to fit in with the crowd and conform to those around us, we are not helping to build up society and the lives of those we impact. It can be intimidating to put yourself out there, especially in the face of criticism and those who aren't willing to accept what you bring to the table. But if you try to conform to the status quo when it goes against who you are and what you believe, then you will never live a fulfilled life.

For some, being your true, authentic self can be intimidating—but it has to be done if you ever want to be happy and reach your goals. If you spend your life worrying so much about what other people think and fail to just be yourself, you are wasting the precious time that you have on this earth.

So be you. Be goofy or serious, be a homebody or a party animal. Be a bookworm or a stud athlete. Be a little bit of all of those things if you want—your life doesn't need to be defined by set categories or boundaries. The world needs all types, but most importantly it needs everyone to be their authentic self. You will find people who love and support the true you, so don't let those who don't appreciate you force you to change who you are.

Choose to be happy. Do what you love and pursue it passionately. Live the existence that you've always envisioned for yourself—write the story of your life and create fulfilling moments each step of the way. You are the main character of your own story—make sure that when you look in the mirror you are the protagonist you want to be.

If your actions don't line up with your thoughts and beliefs, then you need to figure out why that is. Are you letting outside forces influence how you act? Are you scared to reveal your true self for fear that others will put you down? Whatever it is, determine the reason for the disconnect and work to resolve it so that you can be your true self.

If you are someone who is already being your authentic self in your life—great! But know that there are still times for most people when their actions don't truly reflect their belief system. You need to know who you are and what you believe in and constantly check in to make sure that your actions reflect this. For example, if you say that you have a strong belief in yourself and your abilities, but constantly use negative self-talk, then your belief system and actions aren't truly in line. Being authentic is a 24/7 thing—not just when it's convenient or easy. Sometimes being your authentic self means sticking up for yourself and your beliefs when it goes against the crowd. Be strong, be you.

Get Up and GRIND

- What are your core beliefs? If you want to be your true self, you need to know what you believe in. Write down the 5-10 core beliefs that help shape the way you interact with the world.
- Do you notice yourself changing the way you act based on who you are around? If so, make a commitment to be your authentic self in all situations—not a chameleon who changes based on the situation.

Hunt Down Opportunity - Say Yes

Opportunities are out there—but you need to hunt them down. And you need to be aware of the fact that sometimes those opportunities don't look as grand as you think they should. There are times, especially when starting out, that you need to take chances and say "yes" to things that may seem like they aren't as big as you'd hoped they would be—but they are stepping stones and much needed experience to get where you want to be.

A common example is with aspiring musicians, taking small gigs is part of the process—you never know who will be in the audience, so you have to make sure you give your full effort. What if there happens to be a music exec at the Podunk bar you're playing at for $50 a night—you better give him a good show, even if you don't know he's there.

But the same premise is true in most endeavors—no matter how small the work you are doing seems to be, you have to approach it like it is the most important opportunity you will have. When you approach your work like this from the beginning, it builds on top of itself and creates a solid foundation to grow on. Those "small gigs" deserve your best efforts, even if you can't see the pay off in the immediate present. You are creating good habits and meaningful experience as you build to your end goal.

If you think you are too good or too big to take opportunities when starting out, you may need to reevaluate why it is you're doing what you're doing. Hopefully your goals align with your passion, and even the smaller gigs fire you up and excite you. It's nice, and important, to profit from the work you do—but you also have to understand that the money may not flow in right away, as much as you'd like it to. When you are starting, taking opportunities for little or no financial compensation may have to be part of the process. This isn't a forever thing—eventually you need to turn your work into a profitable endeavor, but at the beginning consider these opportunities as continued education. The time you spend at the beginning of your new career or endeavor learning and gaining experience will likely lead to enhanced success in the future.

If you need some more convincing on this, take some time and read biographies of those who you view as the ultimate successes in their field. Chances are you'll find a common theme—they put in their time at the bottom, gaining experience, and maybe even had to eat some ramen noodles along the way. But their passion fueled them. They jumped at opportunities, and the lessons learned from their experiences guided them to the success they attained.

If you're further along in your career and your journey, remember that it's never too late to put yourself out there and seek more opportunities and knowledge. For you it may not mean low paying gigs and being the bottom rung on the totem pole, but it could mean investing your valued and limited time into your continued growth. No matter where we are in our personal and professional lives we can't become stagnant and stop pursuing opportunities for growth. Everyone is busy, and it's easy to get stuck in your daily routine without expanding your horizons—especially if you've already reached some level of success. Create a network of others whose work you respect and share your insights with each other. Look to people in fields other than your own who you admire and see what you can learn from them. Especially in today's constantly changing world, you can never become complacent with what you know and what you are doing. Always be learning and growing, or expect others to pass you by.

Whatever level you're at, just starting out or already living a successful life, realize that you can't just expect opportunities to come knocking at your door. Be willing to go hunt them down. Identify the people in your field who are doing what you want to do and begin to study them. Find out their back-story, follow them on social media, and even reach out to them for advice. They didn't get to where they are by accident, and a lot can be learned from those who have already achieved success. Follow your gut and take chances. Be yourself and be open to learn from people in all different fields. We aren't on this journey alone, and the more information and advice you can learn from others, the better off your own journey will be.

Get Up and GRIND

➢ Are you open to the limitless opportunities available to you, or are you in the habit of saying "no" to new experiences and chances to learn in your field? This week, find and say yes to one new opportunity that will make you better at what you do.

Fake It 'Til You Make It

You can't expect others to believe in you and take you seriously if you don't believe in yourself. Regardless of the endeavor we're discussing, if you want to be successful, you have to exude a confidence and belief in self that will give others the confidence to believe in you as well.

We all have moments of doubt, but you need to be able to put that doubt aside and put on an aura of self-assurance and conviction that lets others know that you know what you're doing. So what do you do if you don't have that self-belief? Fake it 'til you make it. Everyone has to start somewhere, including those who you now see at the top. They didn't start there, but more than likely they believed in who they were and what they were doing and they worked their way up. Yes, you need to be your authentic self—but if that self is riddled with self-doubt, then you need to quiet those thoughts and recalibrate your thinking to one of assured confidence. Act like you're confident long enough, and chances are somewhere along the way you'll gain the confidence you need to back it up.

This is not to say you should be cocky or a know it all, but it is ok to be sure of yourself. No one wants to hire or be led by someone who waivers on their beliefs or acts like they don't know or have confidence in what they're doing. We want to have faith in our leaders—so our leaders better have faith in themselves first.

What you think has a large impact on what you do and the success you will, or won't, attain. Negative self-talk rarely leads to positive results, whereas embracing a winner's mentality leads to more victories along the way. Approach your daily tasks working toward your goals with an optimistic and assured mindset, knowing that the work you put in now is getting you ever closer to your goal. If you let doubt and uncertainty creep into your daily work, then you are hindering your progress. Believe that the work you are putting in is leading in the right direction, and go about your life with a knowledge that you are putting your best foot forward.

Continue learning and be open to new growth opportunities—be willing to put yourself in situations that you may be under qualified for on paper, but that you have the confidence and determination to take on and learn from along the way. Getting outside of your comfort zone and being willing to put yourself in uncomfortable situations is one of the best ways to experience progress. If you only ever do what you know and are comfortable with, then your development will be stagnant. It's in those situations where you are tested and forced to adapt where the growth occurs. But you need to have the confidence in yourself to put yourself in those situations, and you need to realize the power of being comfortable being uncomfortable. It seems counterintuitive—society screams at us in all directions that we want lives of luxury and ease. And although perhaps that is true in the long term, don't expect to get there without some discomfort and strife along the way. To get to where you want to be, you have to put in the work doing things that are challenging and may at times scare you—do them anyway. It's in the battle over discomfort that we see the most powerful breakthroughs and take the biggest leaps toward excellence.

Get Up and GRIND

➢ In what areas do you lack self-confidence? What positive thoughts or mantras can you fill your head with when those feelings of self-doubt creep into your mind? Create a plan to overcome doubt and execute it anytime your assurance waivers.

➢ Are you comfortable being uncomfortable? Cultivate an understanding of the potential value of discomfort, and next time you encounter discomfort that could lead to growth, do not shy away from it.

The Golden Rule

Maybe this goes without saying, at least hopefully it should—be a good person. Be kind, be helpful, treat others how you want to be treated, and show people respect. These are lessons that we learn in our earliest days of school, and hopefully they don't get forgotten along the way.

It's great to strive for success and to want to be the best at what you do, but remember that people are far more likely to remember how you treated them and made them feel, rather than be impressed with what your profession is or the accolades you've racked up. No goal or achievement is worth losing sight of this, and the reality is that you are more likely to gather support and success if you show a positive and kind attitude to those around you anyway. No one likes conceited, unkind people—and people are less likely to support your goals and assist you if you behave like an asshole.

We all have our good days and bad days, but we can't lose sight of the impact that we have on others, and we need to work every day to ensure that the influence we have on those we interact with is a positive one. When you are feeling particularly irritable, be sure to take time to calm down and gather yourself before interacting with others. They are not going to be impressed if you lose your temper and lash out. If you're someone who is prone to bouts of anger, find ways to manage it and work on being calm and staying in control no matter what situation comes your way. We all have our moments, but it's important to always remember to treat those around you with care and respect.

Remember, too, that we can never know what is going on in somebody's life. Everyone has a story, and the interactions you have with people are just a small part of that. If someone is being short with you or unreasonable, recognize that this could have nothing to do with you—in all likelihood they probably have other issues they are dealing with. Being patient with people and occasionally cutting them some slack does not make you weak, it just makes you compassionate. Strive to give people the benefit of the doubt, and think the best of people. You never know where people are coming from, and taking the time to better understand them will likely help both of your causes.

You get what you put out into the world—so if you want to be treated with respect, cut some slack when you need it, and treated with kindness and dignity—then do the same to others, no matter their social status or how you think they can assist you. This isn't rocket science, but if you want to be happy and successful, it's probably one of the greatest lessons you can remember.

Get Up and GRIND

➢ Make a special effort to be kind to those in your life who have a tendency to aggravate you. Next time you lose your patience with someone, remember that we don't always know what's going on in someone's life, and offer them additional patience and kindness.

Just a Scrapper Livin' the Dream

This last chapter is a little different than the others; it is a brief background into who I am and how following the ideals of the GRIND have shaped my life. We're all on our own paths, but I hope hearing my story can help you on your journey. It should also offer you some insight into why I believe so strongly in the philosophy of "get up, show up, and GRIND," and why I believe that following the GRIND lifestyle is a major key to success. In a world where we are exposed to so many success stories on TV and in the movies, it can become too easy to look at those people and assume they have something we don't have—extra talent, money, good looks, etc. But in many cases what they possess that others don't is an extreme work ethic, and this is what we have to remember as we create our own stories. I hope that "Grind: Greatness Rises In each New Day" helps shape your own story and leads you to success through living the GRIND.

PEOPLE HAVE MANY DIFFERENT VERSIONS of what success looks like. One that resonates with me is from Maya Angelou, who says "Success is liking yourself, liking what you do, and liking how you do it." Ultimately, I believe that a big part of being truly successful is living the life you've always dreamed of. Although my life may not be the one others aspire to—it is a better life than I could have ever imagined for myself. I make a living doing something I absolutely love, I spend my days training and coaching others to be the best versions of themselves, and I have real satisfaction in my day-to-day living. None of this would have been possible without the support of those around me, and my willingness to work for what I wanted.

I live the GRIND lifestyle, but I didn't choose the GRIND—the GRIND chose me. Or rather, the GRIND presented itself to me, and I could either accept that showing up and working hard was the way I was going to achieve my goals and dreams, or I could face the reality that based on my raw talent alone there was just no way that I was going to live the life I imagined, or reach the goals I set out to.

Growing up in school I did well, but it never necessarily came easily—it seemed like I was constantly studying and doing homework. While others were partying, skipping class, and doing just enough to get by, I felt like I always had to be working in order to earn the grades I wanted. But I was committed to excellence, put in the work I had to, and graduated high school with a 4.2 GPA. I was accepted to the College of the Holy Cross, and headed there to study and play ice hockey. Hockey was much the same way—I was never the star but was so passionate about the game that I practiced and played incessantly. During high school my dream was to play college hockey, so I got on every sheet of ice I could, shot thousands of pucks in my backyard, stickhandled hours a day, and wrote training programs for myself that I hoped would put me in the best physical shape I could be in to compete. Although I didn't start playing the game until I was in eighth grade, which in the world of hockey is quite late, I was able to achieve my dream of playing in college. While I was there, I continued working hard and managed to put together four years of collegiate-level hockey, of which I am very proud—I was never the star player, but was happy to be playing the game I loved for a school that I loved. There were moments where the stress and level of commitment didn't seem worth it, but in the end, the lessons I learned set me up for the next phases of my life. There is no way I would have been able to play collegiate hockey on talent alone... I just wasn't good enough. It was my passion for the game and my work ethic that helped me realize this dream, not my hockey skills or innate talent.

After I graduated from Holy Cross, I continued my education by entering a program that allowed me to get my masters in education and teach full time. The program was based out of Creighton University in Omaha, Nebraska and I taught in Rapid City, South Dakota. For a girl from Cape Cod, Massachusetts this was quite the change—but I was ready for an adventure. At 22 with no teaching experience and thrown into the classroom, adventure is exactly what I got. But perhaps the greatest lessons I learned came from my time coaching ice hockey, track, and high school football. With no previous experience in coaching football, I became the first female football coach in the state of South Dakota. How did this happen? After two years of teaching in the school, I continued to be so impressed with the football team—not just for their winning record, but more so for the way that the young men on the team carried themselves, respected their coaches and teachers, and believed in their football program. So in the spring I went to the head football coach, Wayne Sullivan, who was also the high school principal and my boss, and asked if it would be possible for me to intern with the coaches on the team in the fall with the goal of learning as much as possible about coaching. I told him that I believed that good coaching translated, no matter the sport, and could see that what they were doing was working and I wanted to learn and be a part of that. To my surprise, he hired me as a football coach on the spot (I use the term "hire" loosely, as I was paid in team gear and experience—but I would take that experience over money any day). Leading up to summer training camp was probably the most nervous and scared I have ever been in my life, even still. I will never forget the feeling I had right before going to the first coaches meeting. I almost turned around and went home. Looking back, I am so grateful that I didn't let fear stop me from doing something that, although unconventional, I knew would help make me a better coach, teacher, and leader. Many of the lessons I learned that season have stuck with me, and I never would have gained that confidence and experience had I let my fear convince me that, because I was a woman, I couldn't coach football.

After my time in South Dakota I returned home with the goal of opening a CrossFit gym. I took an unpaid internship with my former strength and conditioning coach, Jeff Oliver, at Holy Cross and became consumed with learning as much as I could about human movement, coaching, and running a gym. I would go to the local CrossFit gym in the morning for a workout then head to the weight room at Holy Cross and begin coaching athletes who were there training for their upcoming seasons. I helped run several coaching sessions a day, and on my time off I would typically get in another workout and/or head to the Holy Cross library, or find a corner of the ice rink and study for the CSCS (Certified Strength and Conditioning Specialist) exam. Having graduated three years earlier, it was odd to be back in the library and rink studying—but I was driven to learn as much as I could and set myself up for success.

That summer, I had a lot of great conversations with the head strength and conditioning coach at Holy Cross, Jeff Oliver (or "Ollie," as we called him), that helped shape and reinforce what I wanted to do. Of all the coaches I have had in my life—he has been the most influential. Ollie is a large man with the biggest hands and heart I've ever seen. He has a way of being incredibly supportive and yet holds you to the highest standard. He values hard work and doesn't tolerate anything less than your best effort. For someone who only gets by through extreme effort and hard work, I appreciated that he noticed those athletes who were willing to show up and GRIND—even if they weren't the star players. No matter who you are he makes you feel valued and important, recognizes your hard work, and pushes you to be your best self. He reinforced for me the notion that coaching, and much of life, is based on relationships. You need to truly care about those people you work with and help them to become better than when they came to you. This has come to be a core value of mine, and Coach Ollie is a perfect role model for me in my attempt to live it out.

After my summer interning in the weight room at Holy Cross, I moved back home to the Cape, where I took a teaching job and began the work of learning the logistics of starting a gym. I began to look for space, write a business plan, and continue to work on how I would be the best coach I could be. On December 26, 2011, I, along with the help and support of my parents and friends, opened CrossFit Hyannis. I remember waking up on that morning not knowing what to expect. It was the day after Christmas and I had done minimal mainstream marketing. I had gotten the message out via social media and gone to all of the local police and fire stations offering them the chance of a free or reduced cost membership, but had no idea who, if anyone, would be there on that first day. Although I was nervous about what was to come, I also believed wholeheartedly in what I was doing and why I was doing it.

The next few months were a whirlwind. I had moved back home to my parents' basement and taken a full-time job teaching middle school to save money as I transitioned into being a gym owner and coach. After seven years living away from home, and at the age of 25, it could have been a blow to my ego to move back home, but I had a bigger long-term vision, and saving money to open the gym was my top priority. I am lucky enough to have parents who supported me in that goal, and let me set up shop in the basement while I worked toward it.

So each day I would wake up at 4:15am to coach the 5:30am class at the gym. From there, I would quickly shower and head to my "real job" down the street teaching middle school. Although I knew that my long-term goal was to be at the gym full time, I also never wanted to short my students of the attention, preparation, or presence that they deserved. So I consumed a lot of caffeine, held impromptu push up competitions in my classroom when the kids (or more likely I) needed a little pick me up, and let my passion carry me. After my teaching day was done, I would head back to the gym, hope to get a quick workout in, and then coach the

4:30, 5:30, and 6:30pm classes. When classes were over, along with the help of my mother, I would stay and mop the floors and clean the gym.

During this time of my life, every free moment I had, when I wasn't actively teaching or coaching, was spent preparing for teaching or coaching. Lesson planning, grading, programming, working on the gym's website or social media, trying to recruit members for my new gym, etc. I told many of my friends at this time to "stick it out" with me as I constantly turned down their invites to hang out, go out to dinner, missed their birthday parties and even weddings. It wasn't that I wanted to miss these things or have my relationships take a back seat—but I knew that in order for the gym to be successful I had to go all in, and the people who truly loved and supported me would stick it out with me (and they did).

After that spring, I didn't go back to teaching and made the plunge into making the gym my full-time job. Looking back, it's hard to imagine how I managed on those long days—especially knowing that most of that time was in front of people, which if you've ever taught or coached, you know how exhausting it can be to always be "on." But the reality is at the time I didn't think twice about it. I was following my dream, and was willing and excited to put in the work necessary to make it successful, even if that meant some short-term sacrifice in the moment.

I always laugh when I hear people say how great my job must be—just working out and coaching all day. And although it truly is great, it doesn't surprise me that people sometimes fail to see all of the behind-the-scenes work and sacrifice that goes into being successful—even if it is doing something that you love. The same thing often happens when people watch sports on TV—they see the glory, but often overlook the countless dedicated hours and years it took to get to that moment.

The gym grew steadily, and two years after opening the gym, at the age of 27, I was awarded a "Top 40 Under 40" award from Cape & Plymouth Business. It was great to share that moment with my friends and family who had believed in my dream and stuck it out with me through those early crazy days, and also the members of the gym who had joined me in creating a great, inspiring, and motivating community. The award was also another reminder to me of the importance of just showing up and working hard—I was being rewarded for doing something that I am passionate about and that I absolutely love to do, but I was only able to do those things because I was willing to make sacrifices and work my ass off. I truly love coaching others, but I also understand that in order to be able to do this, it's necessary to do a lot of tasks that aren't quite as fun too. People may want to believe that owning a gym is a dream job where you just work out and coach all day, guzzling protein shakes and having flex offs in your spare time. But the reality is that a lot goes on behind the scenes of any successful endeavor, and it's only those willing to make sacrifices, show up, and go all in that are going to make it.

Now, over four years into running the gym, it has become an amazing community of people who are dedicated to getting better every day. Due to our location on Cape Cod, a frequent vacation spot for New Englanders, and people from all over the world, each summer we have hundreds of visitors who come train with us and join in our community. I no longer have to clean the gym or coach every class, but there are still countless little tasks to accomplish in order to be successful and continue to grow my business and have a positive impact on people's lives. The best part of my day is that I get to see people every day who live out the concepts in this book—people who aren't afraid to work hard for what they want and attack challenges each day with the goal of bettering themselves.

These are just some of the broad brushstrokes of my life. The truth is, the essence of the GRIND is found in the little decisions that we make everyday—and it's those decisions that lead to painting the bigger pictures of our lives. Every decision I make isn't perfect, and there are definitely days when I want to be lazy—that's normal. We all need motivation along the way, and I hope this book offers you that.

The ultimate premise of "GRIND: Greatness Rises In each New Day" is that in order to achieve greatness and success, you have to be willing to put in the work—you have to be ready to GRIND. In all of my experiences up to this point in my life, this is the overwhelming factor that I have noticed that distinguishes those who experience success and fulfillment and those who are never satisfied, often living in fear (fear of rejection, failure, of living a mediocre life, etc.). When people tell me that they want to lose weight but then never show up to the gym, it drives me crazy. When someone says that they hate their job but never even look for other opportunities, I wonder what they're waiting for. They are missing the first step—SHOW UP. What you are hoping for is almost certainly not going to happen overnight, but it's never going to happen if you don't take the first step.

I don't think the life of a business owner/entrepreneur is for everyone, but the GRIND philosophy goes far beyond just owning a business. If you are pursuing what you are truly passionate about, no matter what it is, it will be hard, and it will be worth it. Whether that's in your life, your business, your relationships, your sport/art, or anything else—they key is showing up and putting in work. Never think you know everything, and always be willing to learn. You never know when you're going to get your big break, but I can almost guarantee you it will never happen if you don't ever show up, work hard, and give it your best effort.

Get Up and GRIND

> What's your story? How do you live out the GRIND principles to live the life you desire?

Now it's time for you to get up, show up, and GRIND. Greatness Rises In each New Day, the book and the company, were created to share our philosophy and to unite those who believe in the value of hard work in all of their endeavors—from their profession, to their social life, hobbies, sport, and beyond. We believe that there's an immeasurable value in working toward what you desire, and we want to bring together a community of people who share this view and are willing to chase down their goals with grit and determination.

We hope you embrace the GRIND lifestyle—never being afraid to work for what you want, refusing to settle for the status quo, and constantly pursuing excellence and greatness. Part of our mission is to support and bring together a community who gets up, shows up, and GRINDS to reach their goals—so share your story with us and inspire others along the way.

And most importantly, remember:
greatness awaits—but you have to go get it.

Visit us at www.greatnessrisesineachnewday.com
and share your story.

About the Author

Katie Falkowski is the owner and head coach of CrossFit Hyannis on Cape Cod, MA where she works with amazing people everyday on their journey to bettering themselves and reaching their goals. She owns the lifestyle/apparel company "GRIND: Greatness Rises In each New Day" whose mission is to inspire, motivate, and connect those on their quest to becoming the best version of themselves through hard work and dedication. In addition to hanging out with her friends and family, her favorite pastimes include working out and eating pizza.

To stay up to date, get continued motivation, and connect with the GRIND community visit us at www.greatnessrisesineachnewday.com.

Made in the USA
San Bernardino, CA
12 June 2016